MEMORIES
OF
WEST BROMWICH

ALTON DOUGLAS
DENNIS MOORE
ADDITIONAL RESEARCH BY JO DOUGLAS.

ISBN 0 947865 05 5

Published by Beacon Broadcasting Ltd., 267 Tettenhall Road, Wolverhampton WV6 ODQ.
Printed by Windmill Printing, Portersfield Road, Cradley Heath, Warley, West Midlands, B64 7BX.

CONTENTS

Mike Cowley and Ian Shorthouse watch as well-known broadcaster Ed Doolan launches into his role as Vice-President of Sandwell Hospital Radio, 25th January 1985.

Betty Boothroyd, MP for West Bromwich West, and Peter Snape, MP for West Bromwich East, hand in their election nomination papers at the Town Hall, 20th May 1983. Both were successful.

West Bromwich Borough Council, 1962/3.

EVENTS

Captain James Eaton, who served under Admiral Lord Nelson, died on 28th February 1857 at his home, Hill House, Dagger Lane. At the Battle of Trafalgar he was a midshipman and had a hand in Nelson's famous signal "England expects that every man this day will do his duty." His grave is in All Saints' churchyard.

In the middle of the 19th century a certain man named Hudson invented a dry soap-powder and had a small factory in West Bromwich prior to opening a larger one in Liverpool, which was taken over by Lever Brothers of Port Sunlight in 1908. Enamel signs advertising Hudson's Soap are treasured as memorabilia.

Farley Park became town property in 1890 when presented by Alderman Farley. The cost of layout and buildings came to £1,699. Four years later the 25 acres of Kenrick Park became another gift to the town, the donors being J. Arthur Kenrick and William Kenrick.

Many people in the town on a June day in 1920 would have been craning their necks to see the British airship R33 cruise slowly over the area.

West Bromwich, Smethwick and District Manufacturers' Association was formed in 1924 with the principal objects of assisting local manufacturers with problems and with creating a spirit of co-operation and mutual help between those manufacturers.

First opened to the public in 1929, Red House Park, on the outskirts near Great Barr, was delightfully wooded, with blue-bells in spring-time.

West Bromwich Operatic Society, which still raises funds for charity, was founded in 1934 by Norman Bassett, son of Billy Bassett, the famous footballer for West Bromwich Albion and England.

In addition to the Freedom of Entry granted to the 1st Battalion, South Staffordshire Regt. on 23rd July 1949, a similar honour was conferred on "Q" (West Bromwich) Battery, Light Anti-Aircraft Regt., RA, TA on 25th July 1959.

The Manor House, Hall Green Road (originating from around 1300)was restored over the period 1957 to 1961 and was then opened as a quality restaurant.

A trip out from Ye Old Fountain Inn, c.1910.

PRESENTATION OF THE

FREEDOM OF THE BOROUGH

AND

. . LUNCHEON . .

TO

Lieut.-Gen. Sir John D. P. French, K.C.B., K.C.M.G.,

ON THE OCCASION OF THE

OPENING OF THE DRILL HALL.

AUGUST 1ST, 1903.

An outing to who-knows-where? c.1920.

West Bromwich Butchers' Outing, c. 1919.

Staff function, Guest Motors, c. 1935.

May Day Parade at the corner of Clive Street, 1936.

The Proclamation, announcing the accession of King George VI, is read by the Mayor, Councillor A.Lellow, 15th December 1936.

Councillor Arthur Smith's Coronation Outing for Old Age Pensioners, May 1937.

The Mayor, Alderman A. Lellow, takes part in the Coronation celebrations, 1937.

Eventful Year for West Bromwich

Drama in the Story of Local War-time Measures

HOW THE TOWN ADAPTED ITSELF

Important Schemes Which Have Had to be Postponed

The outstanding impression gained from surveying the life of West Bromwich during the past year is that all branches of activity have adapted themselves most readily to the new conditions imposed by the war. September 3rd is the date dividing two distinct phases in local affairs, yet in surveying the year as a whole one can see that from early spring events had begun to lead up to a climax.

It was in March that the great "drive" in national service began. The newly-appointed committee for national service were soon chafing under their lack of executive power, but the A.R.P. recruiting campaign, which was launched in the town in the following month, met with an enthusiastic response. It was the biggest campaign of the kind the town had seen, and from that time civil defence work became the dominant feature of local affairs. In May, further developments in the arrangements for the protection of the town were announced; in June, the Council accepted a limited measure of evacuation granted to the town after strong representation had been made in London; in July, it was decided to spend £3,000 on strengthening basements to accommodate 2,000 people in the event of air raids.

At the beginning of August, there were strong protests against the irksome Home Office delays which were affecting the council's A.R.P. proposals—then the storm broke.

The local events immediately preceding and following Britain's declaration of war appear, perhaps, even more dramatic in perspective than they did at the time. At the end of August, important meetings of A.R.P. and A.F.S. volunteers were held, and the Town Clerk (Mr. G. F. Darlow) made an urgent appeal for the co-operation of the townspeople in all civil defence measures. Every effort was being made to provide as much public shelter as possible, and there was feverish activity in working out a scheme for the evacuation of school-children. Immediately war was declared the civil defence services sprang to life, and quickly established an efficient routine. Respirators and helmets for babies were distributed; evacuation was completed without a hitch, though the response of parents was disappointing; committees for the control of food and fuel were set up, and, more recently, the Mayor's committee for comforts for the troops began its good work.

THE ROYAL VISIT.

That is one phase, the more vital phase of the town's life—now let us look back upon the pre-war months. It is sad reflection in the sense that so much that was begun has now been shelved because of the war. The outstanding memory is of the in building houses during the past 20 years.

In the following month the Council approved a £127,140 scheme for the complete reconstruction of the main road from the Hawthorns boundary to the boundaries at Tipton and Wednesbury (it will be recalled that the tram services on these routes were superseded by 'buses in April), but this ambitious plan has, of course, had to be shelved now, though part of it, to cost £6,492, will be proceeded with. This sum will be found out of current estimates, so the Council decided a few weeks ago to do the best they could with it—the removal of the whole of the tram tracks and the reconstruction of the road between New Street and Bull Street.

In August, the provision of children's playing equipment in all parks without it was promised by Councillor A. Guest (chairman of the Estates Committee) when members of the Council made the annual tour of the parks and recreation grounds.

EDUCATION.

The serious effect of the war and evacuation on the work of the Education Committee is only too apparent in looking back over the past twelve months. In February, estimates amounting to £157,100 for elementary education and £28,289 for higher education were approved. Both departments announced considerably less expenditure during the past year than was budgeted for.

At the same time, however, it was revealed that owing to the necessity for revising the plans for completion of the Kenrick Technical College, the estimates for the scheme had "jumped" by £11,720 to £59,935. This increase led to protests, but it is of no consequence now, for the completion cannot be proceeded with owing to the war.

Since July, practically all the important work of the committee has had reference to civil defence. In that month a scheme of air raid protection for 7,000 school-children and staff was approved at an estimated cost of £20,200. Later came the announcement that West Bromwich had been granted a limited measure of evacuation, and then with the war upon us, work was rushed forward on shelters at schools in the "neutral" part of the town. As this work has been completed, the schools have been opened, and it was most gratifying to learn at the beginning of December that the Grammar School and the Junior Art and Technical Schools will be opened in the New Year.

December 1939

POLICE BALL

Enjoyable Event at West Bromwich

Those who are acquainted with the police only when they are on duty miss something. At the annual West Bromwich Police Ball at the Town Hall on Wednesday, members of the Force and a host of friends enjoyed themselves immensely in an evening of revelry, the proceeds of which are to be devoted to police charities.

There were about 500 people present, and if the floor was sometimes over-crowded there was much to compensate for this slight discomfort. Novelties and paper hats were introduced, and there was plenty of variety in the dances.

The M.C. was Mr. Arthur Hayward, and the music was supplied by Den Bannister and his band.

Among those who attended were the Mayor and Mayoress (Councillor E. Woodward and Mrs. Thornton), the Deputy Mayor and Mayoress (Councillor and Mrs. H. Bellingham), Alderman C. B. Adams, Mr. G. F. Darlow (Town Clerk), Mr. J. G. Jefferson (Borough Surveyor), Mr. H. Clarke (Magistrates' Clerk's Department) Superintendent and Mrs. C. A. Clarke, Dr and Mrs. G. Clarke, and Miss N. Clarke.

8.5.45.

The case of Poland

THE *Evening Despatch* is to be congratulated on its leading article, which puts the Russian-Polish question in its proper perspective. Mr. Chas. E. Smith walks on dangerous ground when he goes back 30 years, and I would remind him that some of us can go back a great deal farther than that.

It is remarkably strange that Soviet Russia — holding the immense territorial surface of the globe that she does—is the only one of the United Nations who wishes to grab any more land, and that at the expense of a smaller and weaker nation.

If Poland fails to get justice but is to have Soviet so-called justice forced upon her, our boys have died in vain.

EX-SOLDIER.

West Bromwich.

The King and Queen visit West Bromwich in 1940. Here they leave the Railway Station with the Mayor, Councillor Edward Woodward, and the Earl of Dudley, the Regional Commissioner for Civil Defence.

The choristers prepare for a trip to Alton Towers from Trinity Methodist Chapel, Great Bridge, 1937.

One of the floats in the Warship Week Parade, Sandwell Road 15th November 1941.

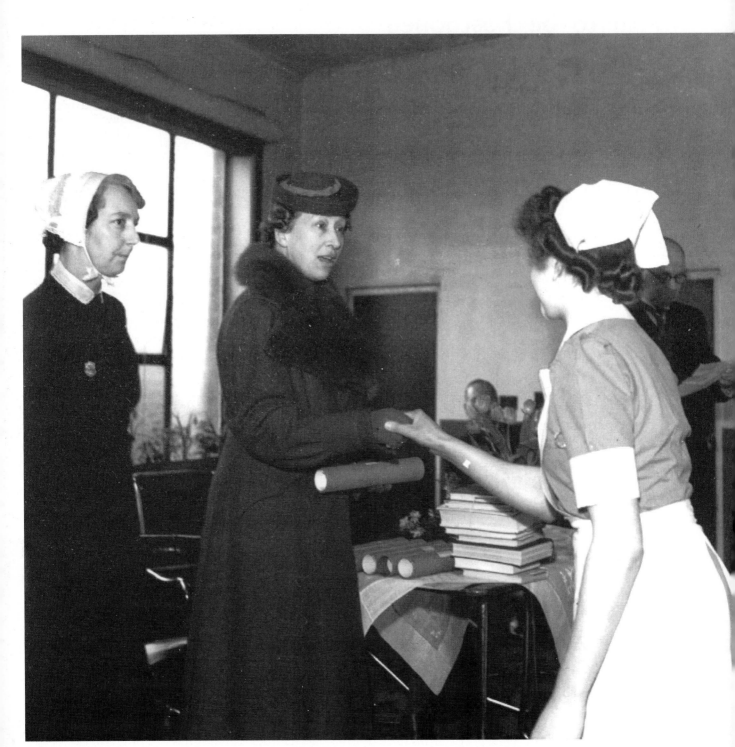

Mary, the Princess Royal, presents awards in connection with the YMCA appeal for the War and National Service Fund, General Hospital, 20th March 1946.

Centenary Luncheon, West Bromwich
Building Society, 23rd April 1949

25

Come listen to the band at the opening of the Garden of Memory, 12th May 1951.

The Rex Cinema, Hill Top, is hired for two days by Mr A. Edwards, to give special film shows for children to celebrate the Coronatio
June 1953.

Coronation Party in the yard of the Plough and Harrow, William Street, June 1953.

Coronation Party, Charlemont School, Holyhead Road, June 1953.

The official opening of new premises of the TSB Bank, 286 High Street, 11th May 1953.

Christmas Party, Phoenix Steel Tube Company, December 1953.

West Bromwich Ladies' Circle No. 214 celebrate the presentation to them of the National Charter at the Sandwell Hotel, 1957.

George Shepherd, inventor of the Shepherd Ball Castor, is presented with a gold-plated set of furniture castors to mark the production of the 1,000,000th castor at Archibald Kenrick &Sons Ltd., Union Street, 1958.

93rd (Dartmouth) West Bromwich Cub Pack prepares to march off on the St. George's Day Parade, 1959.

The Mayor, Alderman Philip Taylor formally declares the Yew Tree Community Centre open, 15th November 1962.

9.6.60

BESIDES being proud of the fact that it is celebrating its bicentenary this year, the world-famous West Bromwich firm of George Salter and Co. Ltd., has another event to commemorate. It has a works social club that has just passed its own century mark and is thus one of the oldest organisations of its kind in the country.

The firm of Salter was founded by a Richard Salter at Bilston in 1760 and moved to West Bromwich between 10 and 20 years later. The works club was started, with a library, recreation room and dining hall, late in 1859

12-acre Social Centre

History was made for this club in 1928 when the recreational activities were transferred to Springfields, West Bromwich, the former Salter family home.

To-day Mr. R. P. S. Bache, chairman and managing director of the company, will link the bicentenary and the centenary. He will take members of the firm's welfare committee to Springfields to see a new bowling green being laid—the firm's bicentenary contribution to the abundant sports facilities already available at the 12-acre social centre.

Another gesture is the granting of a day's holiday to all employees on June 20.

Prince Philip visits Lodge Road Youth Centre, 28th March 1969.

1971

MORE than 250 children of Metal Closures employees, attended a Christmas party at the firm's canteen on Saturday at Bromford Lane, West Bromwich.

It was organised by the Sports and Social Club, under the chairmanship of Mr. L. G. Great-batch.

Seventeen children took part in a fancy dress competition, which was won by Mandy Darby, dressed as Little Bo Peep.

Second was Margaret Starkey (a clock) and third was Adrian Morris (a letter box).

The climax of the party was the arrival of Father Christmas.

Members of West Bromwich Central Townswomen's Guild visit the floral clock in Dartmouth Park designed to mark their 25th anniversary, 9th August 1972.

Christmas Party at George Salter's Social Club, Roebuck Lane, 22nd December 1970.

Six new Freemen are installed by the Mayor and Mayoress, Alderman and Mrs Ernest Knight, 19th May 1970.

Chairman and M.D., Mrs C. I. Taylor, helps to celebrate the 50th anniversary of her company Hall Brothers (West Bromwich) Ltd., by presenting a long-time award to J. H. Benfield, 30th October 1972.

The foundation stone of the £80,000 All Saints' Church of England Primary School is laid by the Archdeacon of Stafford, the Ven. Basil Stratton, 2nd November 1972.

John Day cuts the ribbon to open the West Bromwich Expressway, 7th May 1973.

The Queen leaves the Oak House, 27th July 1977.

33

Albion Starlet Majorettes, Hill Top Carnival, 10th June 1978.

A touch of the Orient at the annual West Bromwich Carnival, 1st July 1978.

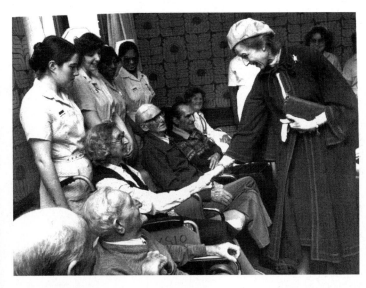

Princess Alexandra meets patients and nurses from Priory Ward, Sandwell District Hospital , November 1980.

Members of the Military Vehicle Conservation Group and the Northern Allied Axis Society advance on shoppers to publicise Sandwell's historical vehicle parade, 21 May 1979.

Princess Margaret, President of the NSPCC, opens the Society's child and family centre at The Elms, High Street, 21st June 1988.

Keith Kelly and Ian Bishop are cheered to the tape, by pupils of Hargate Primary School, as they complete a 4,000 miles sponsored drive around Britain, 27th April 1989. Along with Ian Nicholls and Derek Jarvis, the ambulancemen were taking part in the "Ambuthon '89" appeal.

AT WORK

Long before the Industrial Revolution (c. 1730 to 1850), West Bromwich was still a village and mainly agricultural. The town's Old Forge began operating in 1735 and when the Wolverhampton to Birmingham canal was opened in 1769, this had the effect of halving the price of coal which was being mined extensively in the district. Old corn-mills became slitting-mills which produced slim iron lengths ready for hand-made nails, a product which brought, West Bromwich much fame. Family industries sprang up and long hours were worked at home, aided only by candlelight when night-time arrived.

By 1834 there were 14 local coachsmiths and, within twenty years, gun-barrels, flintlocks and pistols were being made.

At Spon Lane, in 1825, the largest gasworks in the kingdom was in production. The whole of the main road from Birmingham to Dartmouth Square was gaslit by 1834. The West Midlands Gas Board took over in 1949.

Electricity was Corporation-supplied in 1898 and, amidst fears of what effect it would have on the gas industry, a generating station was constructed at Black Lake (originally known as Blake Lake). The Midlands Electricity Board took control in 1943.

Now, no coal is mined in the West Bromwich area but other industries have grown instead, namely mining-plant, steel for bridges, forgings, castings, springs, nuts & bolts, metal windows, car & aircraft components, switchgear, heating & ventilation units, disinfectants, oils, acids, printing & stationery, hand-tools, hollow-ware and many more.

Sinking of a shaft at Jubilee Colliery, c. 1907.

A slight pause for the camera and then work continues on the Tantany Estate, 1920.

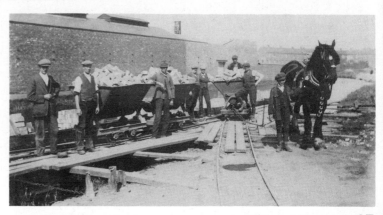

EXPANSION through mechanisation without redundancy . . . That is one of the aims of the Sandwell Casting Company, West Bromwich, in installing a £60,000 electrically-controlled non-ferrous alloy foundry, which the Mayor, Coun. Thomas Rochelle, is to open to-day.

The Mayor, himself a moulder employed by a West Bromwich ironfoundry, will be asked to make the first mould with the plant running at full capacity. He has know-ledge of mechanised foundry practice but this will be a new experience for him since he will merely have to press a lever here, touch a button there and let the "robot" do the rest.

Installation of the new plant marks the most important of a series of developments by a go-ahead firm that has extended its works several times since the war yet maintained production and a high standard of work while reorganisation has been under way.

26.2.59

The opening of the new Hill Top offices of J. Brockhouse & Co. Ltd., 23rd June 1938. The company, now Brockhouse Forgings Ltd., is presently situated in Howard Street..

Contestants in the West Bromwich YMCA squash tournament, 4th January 1981.

Marathon runners at Carters Green Island, 13th July 1981.

Members of West Bromwich (Dartmouth) Cycling Club set off on an informal spin, 1948.

WEST BROMWICH
RAMBLERS

THERE was a good turn-out for Sunday's ramble Cannock Chase and 33 member travelled to Broadhurst Gree by car.

The ramble started from the German Military Cemeter there and, led by Bill Perry, the ramblers walked down the beautiful Sherbrook Valle past the Sherbrook pools.

After a break for elevense at Marquis's Drive they contin ued through Haywood Slad and joined the Nature Trail nea Seven Springs, which took the to the Stepping Stones. From there it was a short walk ove Oat Hill to Milford Commo where lunch was taken.

The afternoon's walk wa through Brocton Coppice an along the top of the hills to th Glacier Stone, which was d posited on the Chase during th last ice-age, from its origin home in the Southern Uplan of Scotland.

The party returned to Broa hurst Green by way of Brocto Field, Pepper Slade and Parr Warren having covered abov 10 miles on a very mild Decem ber day.

10.12.71

GALA BATHS

SWIMMING · DANCING

29.6.32.
WEST BROMWICH
A NEEDLE FIGHT
Boy Edge and Jerry O'Neil
Too Anxious to Win

An outstanding feature in one of the contests the Palais de Danse was the inability of one of t chief seconds to minister in proper style to b charge.

It is high time that a second when acquiring B.B.B. of C. Licence should be required to furni proof of his ability to minister to the wants of h principal.

On this occasion it was very noticeable that t official had not the least idea what to do, whe his man returned to his corner for the usu minute's interval. He would use the rough tow when a sponge was needed, and the boy alwa had to ask for what he required.

I have no doubt that the second was quite co scientious; in fact, it was his enthusiasm th obviously put him off his work, in spite of t "withering looks" cast in his direction by officials employed by the promoters, whose duti were confined to "swinging the towel."

Edge and O'Neil Draw.

Boy Edge (Birmingham), the Southern Area f weight champion, and Jerry O'Neil (Merthy fought a draw in the principal twelve roun contest.

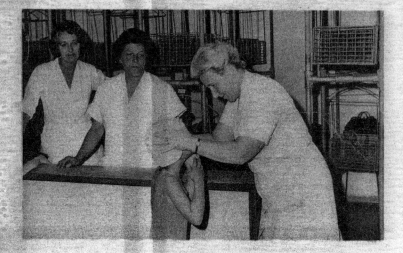

6.10.64.
£60,000 SCHEME PROPOSED
West Bromwich council approves pony trotting plan

The idea of a pony trotting track and sports stadium at Forge-lane was approved in principle by West Brom wich Town Council last night. A move to defer a decision was defeated, only five members being in favour of the deferment.

The Ladies' Changing Room, when the old basket syste was in use, Gala Baths (New Pool), 1972.

Judo action at the Transport Social Club, 27th November 1956.

A Keep-Fit Display entertains the Darby and Joan Club members, Grant Hall, 9th May 1956.

61

WEST BROMWICH OPERATIC SOCIETY

Affiliated to the National Operatic and Dramatic Association

presents

ANNIE GET YOUR GUN

(By arrangement with EMILE LITTLER in Association with CHAPPELL & CO., LTD.)

Music and Lyrics by IRVING BERLIN

Book by HERBERT and DOROTHY FIELDS

at the

KINGS THEATRE

WEST BROMWICH

WEEK COMMENCING

Monday, 3rd November, 1969

FOR FIVE NIGHTS AT 7.15 P.M.   SATURDAY AT 5.0 P.M. & 8.15

PLAZA THEATRE

WEST BROMWICH   Phone: 0030

Directors: R. F. KENNEDY, M. B. KENNEDY, Dudley Hippodrome Ltd.

Licensee	ROBERT F. KENNEDY
House Manager	ROBERT HOPE
Musical Director	DOLPH THOMPSON
Publicity	GEORGE BARTRAM PUBLICITY
Stage Manager	JACK MARR

Box Office open 10 a.m. to 9 p.m

Week Commencing Monday, April 11th, 1955.

1. **OVERTURE**

2. **THE RENEE VENMORE GIRLS**
   Putting on their Top Hats.

3. **MURRAY SMITH**
   The Modern Deceptionist.

4. **O'KEEFE BROS. and ANNETTE**
   Wonder Balancers.

5. **THE RENEE VENMORE GIRLS**
   Presenting the "Doll."

6. **DENNIS LAWES**
   On Laughter Service.

7. **MARGO HENDERSON and SAM KEMP**
   The Essence of Versatility.

8. **INTERMISSION** by the Theatre Orchestra under the
   direction of DOLPH THOMPSON

9. **THE RENEE VENMORE GIRLS**
   All at Sea.

10. **RONDART**
    The Modern William Tell.

11. **THE RENEE VENMORE GIRLS**
    Dancing to Delight.

12. **JOE DEVOE**
    Comic Juggler.

13. **TOMMY FIELDS**
    The Popular Radio, T.V. and Stage Comedian.

    THE QUEEN.

This programme is subject to alteration

LICENSED BAR IN CIRCLE FOYER

NOTICE—PHOTOGRAPHY IN THEATRE FORBIDDEN. Productions being the copyright of the Theatre Proprietors or Producers, the unauthorised photographing of scenes, incidents and acts is illegal.

The Management cannot be responsible for the absence of any artiste through illness or any other circumstances.

Permanent bookings must be claimed one week ahead. When booking in advance MAKE SURE YOUR TICKETS ARE WHAT YOU ASKED FOR. The Manager cannot refund money or give you other seats on tickets which have expired.

In accordance with the requirements of the Watch Committee—

(a) The public may leave at the end of the performance by all exits and entrances other than those used as queue waiting rooms, and the doors of such exits and entrances shall at the time be open.

(b) All gangways, passages and staircases shall be kept entirely free from chairs or any other obstructions.

(c) Persons shall not be permitted to sit or stand in any of the intersecting gangways If Standing be permitted at the rear of the seating, sufficient space shall be left for persons to pass easily to and fro.

(d) The fire-proof curtain shall at all times be maintained in working order and shall be lowered at the beginning of and during the time of every performance.

The Management reserve the right to refuse admission. No re-admission.

"Nina Rosa", Plaza Theatre, performed by the West Bromwich Operatic Society, February 1948.

The Lodge Theatre Society celebrate their 25th anniversary with a production of "Viva Mexico", at the Community Centre, Gayton Road, 23rd April 1983.

July 1938 saw the Clifton, Stone Cross joining the scene. "The Thomson-Houston sound system which has been installed in this theatre reproduces a range of sound frequencies which ensure that every vocal and tonal quality is heard exactly as in the original," they said.

Valerie Hobson opened it and Eddie Cantor was the star of the first film — "Whoopee."

64

Madeleine Carroll, plays the part of a British spy engaged in espionage in war-time Switzerland in "Secret Agent", with John Gielgud, Peter Lorre and Robert Young, 1936.

Tower Cinema, High Street, c. 1965.

- and Alf Garnett lives on today - as he did in 1968!

Imperial Cinema, Spon Lane, May 1975, just prior to demolition.

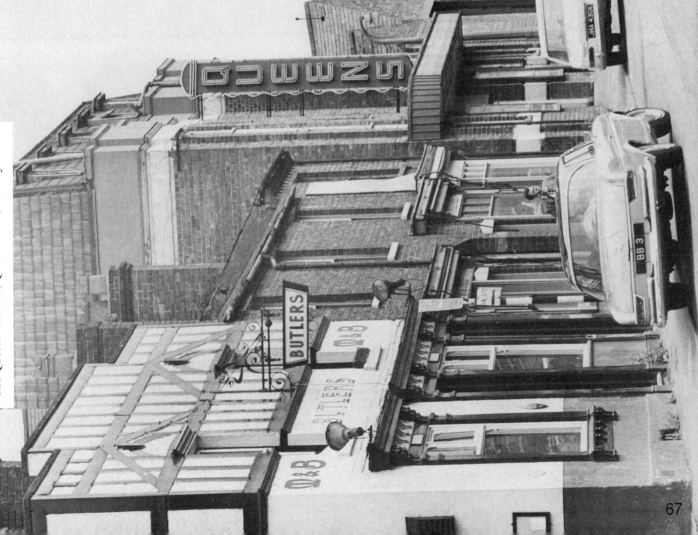

The Queens Cinema, Queen Street, 1st July 1969.

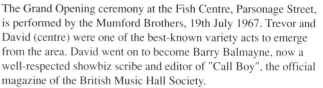

The Grand Opening ceremony at the Fish Centre, Parsonage Street, is performed by the Mumford Brothers, 19th July 1967. Trevor and David (centre) were one of the best-known variety acts to emerge from the area. David went on to become Barry Balmayne, now a well-respected showbiz scribe and editor of "Call Boy", the official magazine of the British Music Hall Society.

Born in Great Bridge, actor Raymond Mason has appeared in such films as "Brannigan" (with John Wayne), "Loophole", "The Best House in London" and "Hearts of Fire". His TV appearances include "The Two Ronnies", "Muck and Brass" and "Boon".

Anne Aston, who for several years was the Golden Girl on ATV's Sunday afternoon programme "The Golden Shot". (Incidentally, Alton, who was the show's warm-up comedian for five years, once compered the show when Norman Vaughan lost his voice.) Her parents ran Hill's Travel and Hill's Coaches and Anne lived in Old Meeting Street from the age of 3 days. Today, she is a successful actress and business woman.

West Bromwich Borough Silver Prize Band, 1933.

West Bromwich Band

celebrates

75 Years

OF MAKING MUSIC
with a
CHRISTMAS CONCERT
at the
GALA RESTAURANT
WEST BROMWICH

Thursday 22nd December

The Springers' Showband, all employed at West Bromwich Spring Company, help to boost the Sandwell scanner fund at a concert at the Sandwell Hotel, June 1979.

Madge Williams and Alan Tomkins, regulars at the Saturday night dances, Gala Hall, 2nd November 1957.

A group of mums, trained by the Joan Hipkiss School of Dancing, gives Olde Tyme Music Hall concerts for charity in the Sandwell area, October 1976.

SANDWELL HOSPITAL RADIO
presents
The Band of the
West Midlands Fire Service
at
WEST BROMWICH TOWN HALL
on
FRIDAY, 6th. APRIL, 1990
Admission 1-50p   Doors open at 6-45p.m.
Refreshments available
Please be seated by 7-20p.m. so as not to interfere
with the live broadcasting of this concert

ON THE MOVE

Joseph Morris drives, with his son George at his side, 1920. Johnson's Rolling Mills are in the background.

In Roman times (55 BC), roads were few and often mere rough, rutted tracks. The only important one to pass near the site of the town was Watling Street, now often referred to as the Holyhead Road. It ran from Dover to Wroxeter in Shropshire. By the mid-17th century, travel was still difficult due to poor roads. A turnpike (a main road with toll-gates), ran from Wednesbury to Birmingham via Hill Top in 1727 and by 1752 the London to Shrewsbury road was re-routed through Carters Green. The journey of 276 miles from London to Holyhead, with a stop at West Bromwich, took 40 hours in 1810. Thomas Telford improved the main road across Bromwich Heath in 1818 and 1826, thus giving added importance to the area. Twenty-one years later, Page's omnibuses were running from Spon Lane to Birmingham three times daily.

Round about this time, The London & North-West Railway began to service the area, and the GWR (Great Western Railway) followed in 1854. By 1860, these railways had almost put the buses out of business.

An act of 1870 allowed West Bromwich the right to build tramways (horse-drawn and steam-driven) but on 31st January 1902 the Corporation decided on electrification and purchased for £32,000 all the sundry-owned tramways in the borough. The decision to withdraw all trams in favour of motor-buses came on 1st January 1939. The original livery was grey and later blue and cream until the West Midlands Authority took over in 1969. The district can still boast one of the finest passenger transport undertakings in the country.

The famous Fellows, Morton & Clayton Co. once had 200 narrowboats plying the local canals, long stretches of waterways set in deep cuttings with embankments dotted with golden broom-bushes which, of course, helped earlier to give the town its name.

INLAND REVENUE.

No. 97

LICENCE.—FOR ONE CARRIAGE AT 15s. 0d.

51 & 52 Vict. cap. 8.

James Coleman Esq
of *15 Sandwell Rd* in the
Parish of WEST BROMWICH. within the
Administrative County* *Boro* of WEST BROMWICH
is hereby authorized to keep ONE CARRIAGE with *less than four wheels*, from the date hereof until the 31st day of December next following; the sum of FIFTEEN SHILLINGS having been paid for this Licence.

Granted at _____
this _____ 4th day of Jan _____ 190 5
by _____ J Scarlett

NOTICE.

This Licence is applicable to a Motor Tricycle, or a Motor Bicycle.

*If the residence is within an Administrative County Borough, insert "Borough".

Sharratt motor-cycles at the factory, Carters Green, c. 1925.

71

Specially-posed group of Crowther Horse Car and South Staffs Steam and Electric Cars at Dartmouth Square, December 1902.

South Staffs Steam Tram, High Street, c. 1900.

The first Electric Tram, 1902

Birmingham and Midland Tramways Car No.2 at Dartmouth Square on the last day of the West Bromwich to West Smethwick route (via Spon Lane), 17th November 1929.

South Staffs Car No.2 outside the Dartmouth Hotel, c. 1904.

Electric trams, Carters Green, 1939.

GOSSIP OF THE WEEK.

MARCH 1939

(BY "THE THROSTLE").

FAREWELL TO TRAMS.

A LITTLE bird whispers to me that the last tram to run through West Bromwich on Saturday night will be given a pretty lively send-off, but what form this will take I have not been able to discover.

* * * * *

Personally, I shall not see (and hear!) the last tram go without a pang of regret. One gets so used to these things, and even tramcars have a certain "following" of enthusiasts, who have a definite, if rather peculiar, affection for them.

* * * * *

However, times change, and forms of transport change with them, and there is little point in being sentimental about a type of vehicle which is fast disappearing in all parts of the country.

* * * * *

Nevertheless, noisy as they may be, they have, over a long period, fulfilled a very useful purpose, and there is something very friendly in the rhythm of the wheels over the joins in the track.

* * * * *

However, we must welcome the 'buses, which should be quite as comfortable and certainly warmer than the tramcars they are to replace.

* * * * *

By the way, I wonder how long it will be before the tram track will follow the trams, and motorists will be able to say that High Street, West Bromwich, is as good a road to travel on as it is to shop in.

* * * * *

THE TRANSPORT CHANGE-OVER.

THE fact that on Sunday next 'buses are to replace the trams at present running through West Bromwich recalls the keen controversy which followed the announcement in the summer of 1937 that the trams were definitely to go. The decision of West Bromwich Town Council in December of the same year to run oil 'buses in place of the trams intensified the difference of opinion as to what form of transport should be used on these important routes. The supporters of trolley 'buses came forward in force, urging the claims of that type of vehicle, and declaring that it was eminently suitable for the routes concerned. The Birmingham and West Bromwich authorities, who are jointly responsible for the services, thought otherwise, however, but in neither Council Chamber was the decision to substitute oil 'buses for the trams reached without some strenuous opposition. All the other authorities through whose "territory" the services run were in agreement with this decision, with the exception of Wednesbury, within whose boundaries, incidentally, is .34 mile of a service the total length of which is 7.454 miles. But Wednesbury, presumably, had their eyes turned in the other direction, there being talk of a proposal to extend Wolverhampton's trolley 'bus services to Wednesbury, and it seemed not impossible that a through service of trolley 'buses from Wolverhampton to Birmingham via West Bromwich and Wednesbury might be established. Whether there was any real foundation or not for that idea, it has certainly gone now. In any case, Birmingham have all along occupied the key position, because, while both Birmingham and West Bromwich have the power to operate motor-'buses in each other's "territory," West Bromwich could not operate trolley 'buses beyond the Handsworth boundary without the permission of the city authorities.

* * * * * 1939

Leyland Tiger Bus, Carters Green Terminus, 1965.

Gordon's Private Hire traditionally convey local F.A. members to the Football Association Vase Final at Wembley each year. On this occasion it was 1986.

Round Table presentation of the first "Books on Wheels" vehicle to the WRVS.

The Birkenhead to London train passes through West Bromwich Station, August 1962.

The Paddington to Birkenhead passes through West Bromwich, August 1962.

TOWN & AROUND

Let us take you through the busy town centre and then go out and about to the green and pleasant parts that are readily accessible.

The High Street is more than 60 feet (19 metres) wide and stretches from Carters Green to Birmingham Road, a total distance of one and a quarter miles (2 kilometres). At its northern end stands the impressive clock tower at Carters Green, close to the district known as Guns Village. It is four-sided and rises to 65 feet (20 metres). Close by stood the Tower Cinema (later to be the ABC) opened on 9th December 1935, having a seating capacity of 2,000. The first film shown was "The Thirty-nine Steps", starring, appropriately, West Bromwich-born Madeleine Carroll. Demolition came in the mid 1980's.

In this area, the famous firm, Jensen Motors Ltd. had their works and in 1934 were fitting motor bodies to quality chassis.

Nearer the centre of things is the Town Hall of pressed brick and stone construction erected over the period 1874/75. It has an imposing tower 130 feet high (40 metres). Now we are at the Library built in 1874 after the Market Hall on the site had been demolished.

Andrew Carnegie, the philanthropist, provided the funds for the new building, amounting to £7,714. A rebuilding project took place in 1907.

The green belt on the eastern side of town, in the region of Mayer's Green and Dartmouth Park, is essential in such a heavily industrialised area. Near here Sandwell Park covers a large acreage and has nature-trails, a farm, woodlands and pools, yet it is totally enclosed by suburbia and the northern arm of the M5 motorway. Here is the site of a medieval Benedictine priory and the location of the Sanctus Fons (Holy Well), giving Sandwell its name.

Sandwell Park Lodge (once the entrance to the Earl of Dartmouth's estate where he occupied Sandwell Hall) stood where the traffic island controls junction 1 of the M5 and Birmingham Road. Now only the archway remains to sometimes puzzle visiting motorists entering the town from the direction of Birmingham.

High Street, 23rd November 1963.

e Public Library, High Street, was erected on the site of the Market Hall. A gift of the philanthropist, Andrew CPOParnegie, it was opened in 1907.

A model railway exhibition, Methodist Schools, High Street, 19th January 1950.

High Street, 24th March 1966.

High Street, c. 1952.

High Street, c. 1955.

Shopkeeper Ron Martin, of New Street, looks on as four-and-half year old Graham Blackwell of St. Clements Lane, with his mother Iris, makes an important pre-bonfire night decision, 30th October 1956.

New Street, 1931.

New Street, 1950.

A barrage balloon over Sandwell Road/ Beale Street, September 1939. Although, today, it seems difficult to believe, they were a very effective part of the anti-aircraft defence system of any town.

84 Looking south east from Carters Green, with High Street running to top of picture. The ABC cinema (now demolished) appears to the right of the Clocktower, 30th September 1968.

Carters Green, 24th March 1970.

Contrasting weather in Sandwell Road, 1952.